Popular Music
Vocals

London College of Music & Media
a faculty of Thames Valley University

Handbook for
Grades One to Eight

Compiled by Anton Browne and Tony Skinner

Printed and bound in Great Britain

Published by **Registry Publications**
Registry House, Churchill Mews, Dennett Road
Croydon   CR0 3JH

ISBN: 1 898466 39 4

Compiled for **LCM Exams** by
Anton Browne and Tony Skinner

Cover design: Bob Burgher
Cover images: Anton Browne

Contents

Introduction

This handbook is designed to accompany the London College of Music grade examination syllabus in popular music vocals. The examination syllabus aims to improve the standards in popular music vocals and provide popular music vocal teachers with a well thought-out and comprehensive structure within which they can teach. Whilst this handbook can be used by students for independent study, it is ideally intended as a supplement to individual or group tuition.

This handbook has been designed with reference to practical music-making situations that are common in popular music: providing a method of studying popular music vocals that is relevant to the practical needs and ambitions of the modern day vocalist.

This handbook covers all five sections of the LCM examinations:

1. MUSICIANSHIP

This chapter enables vocalists to acquire a knowledge of scales and arpeggios: enabling them to become more rounded musicians.

2. PERFORMANCE

This chapter explains the main singing section of the exam, during which candidates perform songs using a 'free choice' of material.

3. MUSICAL KNOWLEDGE (FOR GRADES 3 TO 8 ONLY)

This chapter gives examples of the types of questions that may be asked in this section of the exam. The aim is to empower vocalists with the ability to communicate freely and effectively with other musicians.

4. AURAL AWARENESS

This chapter aims to encourage candidates to develop a good ear for music, enabling them to hear and reproduce rhythms, phrases and harmony lines, and to recognise chords, intervals, time signatures, and cadential movements.

5. SPECIALISMS (FOR GRADES 6, 7 AND 8 ONLY)

This chapter explains the final section of the exam, which allows candidates the opportunity to display their skills in either sight-singing or improvisation.

Musicianship

The purpose of this section of the exam is to encourage the candidate to acquire a 'practical' working knowledge of scales, arpeggios and intervals. This will enable the candidate to become a more rounded *musician*: empowering the candidate with the ability to communicate effectively and knowledgeably with other musicians.

The practice of scales, arpeggios and intervals enables the singer to concentrate on the 'technical' aspects of singing, without having to be concerned with lyrics and the complexities of phrasing, dynamics, etc. In order to facilitate singing scales, arpeggios and intervals it is important to internalise the sound of each scale or arpeggio until you can 'hear it in your head'. In the exam, all scales, arpeggios and intervals must be sung from memory – without reference to this handbook or any other study aid.

TECHNIQUE

The scale and arpeggio requirements listed in this section of the exam are not intended to replace warm-up and breath exercises – these are left to the discretion of the teacher to decide for the individual student, and are not prescribed by the examination board.

Whilst the philosophy of LCM Exams is to assess the *musical result* of technique, rather than technique itself, throughout the exam candidates will be expected to demonstrate:

- a technique that is at least sufficiently stress-free for the vocal mechanism to survive repeated performances;

- a lack of strain on the vocal mechanism, and general lack of muscular tension – particularly in the neck and jaw;

- sufficient vocal range with well-managed register changes;

- good use of the diaphragm and abdominal muscles, resulting in a manner of breathing that is relaxed and yet provides support for the voice over its entire range – with the ability to sustain long phrases.

CHOOSING KEYS

The key/pitch that each scale or arpeggio is performed in should be chosen by the candidate. In this handbook, for reasons of consistency, the scales and arpeggios are all written out in C major or C minor – but remember that you may sing them at any pitch you choose during the exam. It is essential that you choose, in advance, a key/pitch that suits your vocal range. The same key need not be chosen for each scale or arpeggio.

When reading the notation for scales, be careful to observe the key signature for the minor scales: for example, C major and C natural minor scales may appear identical until you notice the key signature.

EXAM CRITERIA

The examiner will be listening for accuracy of the scales or arpeggios themselves and for accuracy of intonation (pitching), but beyond that a musical sound is desirable. This should include:

- Good breath management: taking sufficient breath to last the exercise and not exhausting the breath on the first few notes; taking clean quick breaths (snatch-breaths) when necessary.

- Even tone and intensity: not getting significantly louder as the pitch gets higher and not fading away on the descent. Whilst 'register changes' are inevitable, a key should be chosen that avoids an obvious or difficult change.

- Controlled onset (attack): avoid a heavy or clumsy start to each exercise.

MAXIMUM MARKS for this section of the exam	
Grades 1 to 5	15
Grades 6 to 8	10

WHAT HAPPENS IN THE EXAM

- The examiner will ask you to perform a *selection* of the scales, arpeggios and (from grade three onwards) intervals that are set for the relevant grade. The examiner may not request to hear all the requirements of the grade.

- You should choose the key/pitch and inform the examiner of your choice.

- The examiner will then provide the tonic note before you sing the scale or arpeggio from *memory*.

PERFORMING SCALES AND ARPEGGIOS

- Each scale or arpeggio should be sung once only, unless the examiner requests a further performance.

- You can use any consonant or vowel sound(s), or sol-fa syllables (such as 'lah'), when singing scales and arpeggios in the exam. Consonant and vowel sounds should be accurate and distinct, and where a single consonant or vowel is used its clarity should be maintained.

- A 'neutral' (non-stylised) voice should be used during this section of the exam, avoiding excessive vibrato.

- From grade 5 onwards, all scales and arpeggios may be requested by the examiner to be sung either 'legato' (very smoothly) or 'articulated' (with a separate onset for each note).

- You will notice that some examples are notated in $\frac{4}{4}$ time whilst others are in $\frac{3}{4}$ time. This is because some scales and arpeggios fit better – in a more musical way and with a more natural sense of phrasing – in one or the other time signature.

TEMPOS

In order to provide some general guidance, *suggested* tempos for scales and arpeggios are given in the table below. However, candidates are free to choose their own tempo within the region of +/- 25% of those suggested.

Grades 1 and 2 – 88 bpm
Grades 3 and 4 – 104 bpm
Grades 5 and 6 – 116 bpm
Grades 7 and 8 – 'Slowly': 60 bpm. 'Standard': 116 bpm. 'Fast': ♪ = 160 bpm.

Intervals can be sung at any reasonable tempo, providing the notes can be heard clearly. A suggested tempo is 66 bpm (when sung as minims).

GRADE ONE

At this grade, scales and arpeggios should be sung ascending only. The tempo should be in the region of 88 bpm.

Major scale – 1 octave ascending only

Major arpeggio – 1 octave ascending only

GRADE TWO

At this grade, scales and arpeggios should be sung either ascending or descending as requested by the examiner. The examiner may request the same scale or arpeggio ascending and then, after a suitable pause, descending.

The tempo should be in the region of 88 bpm.

Major scale – 1 octave ascending only

Major scale – 1 octave descending only

Major arpeggio – 1 octave ascending only

Major arpeggio – 1 octave descending only

GRADE THREE

At this grade, scales and arpeggios should be sung ascending and descending without a pause. The tempo should be in the region of 104 bpm.

Intervals should be sung ascending only.

Major scale – 1 octave ascending and descending (without a break)

Major 7th arpeggio – 1 octave ascending and descending (without a break)

Intervals: **Major 3rd**   **Perfect 5th**

GRADE FOUR

At this grade, scales and arpeggios should be sung either ascending or descending as requested by the examiner. The examiner may request the same scale or arpeggio ascending and then, after a suitable pause, descending. The tempo should be in the region of 104 bpm.

Take care to observe the key signature of the natural minor scale.

Intervals should be sung ascending only.

Natural Minor scale – 1 octave ascending

Natural Minor scale – 1 octave descending

Minor arpeggio – 1 octave ascending

Minor arpeggio – 1 octave descending

Intervals: **Major 2nd**   **Major 3rd**   **Perfect 4th**   **Perfect 5th**

GRADE FIVE

- The natural minor scale and minor 7th arpeggio should be sung ascending and descending *without* a pause.

- Take care to observe the key signature of the natural minor scale.

- The major arpeggio should be sung ascending, up to the 5th only; this last note should then be sustained.

- The tempo for scales and arpeggios should be in the region of 116 bpm.

- Scales and arpeggios may be requested by the examiner to be sung either 'legato' (very smoothly) or 'articulated' (with a separate onset for each note).

- Intervals should be sung ascending only.

Natural Minor scale – 1 octave ascending and descending (without a break)

Major arpeggio – up to the 5th with the 5th sustained

Minor 7th arpeggio – 1 octave ascending and descending (without a break)

Intervals:

GRADE SIX

- The major and natural minor scale should begin with an octave jump, before being sung descending. The first (tonic) note of the scale can be held if desired.

- Take care to observe the key signature of the natural minor scale.

- The major arpeggio should be sung ascending only, with the octave note sustained.

- The dominant seventh arpeggio should be sung ascending and descending without a pause.

- The tempo for scales and arpeggios should be in the region of 116 bpm.

- Scales and arpeggios may be requested by the examiner to be sung either 'legato' (very smoothly) or 'articulated' (with a separate onset for each note).

- Intervals should be sung ascending only.

Major scale – octave jump from the tonic and then descending 1 octave

Natural Minor scale – octave jump from the tonic and then descending 1 octave

Major arpeggio – up to the 8th with the 8th sustained

Dominant 7th arpeggio – 1 octave ascending and descending (without a break)

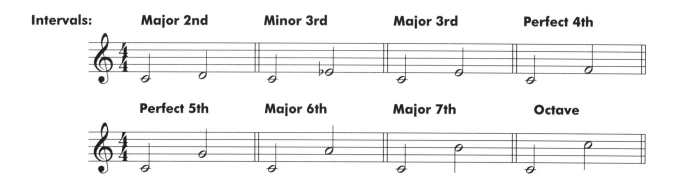

Intervals: Major 2nd   Minor 3rd   Major 3rd   Perfect 4th

Perfect 5th   Major 6th   Major 7th   Octave

GRADE SEVEN

- The major and natural minor scale should be sung ascending and descending slowly, and then (after a short pause) ascending and descending at a fast tempo.

- The blues scale should be sung ascending and descending.

- The major arpeggio should be sung ascending only and then followed immediately (without a pause) by the major scale descending. If desired, the arpeggio notes can be held longer than the scale notes.

- Scales and arpeggios may be requested by the examiner to be sung either 'legato' (very smoothly) or 'articulated' (with a separate onset for each note).

- Intervals should be sung ascending only.

Major scale – ascending and descending 1 octave – first very slowly (with a snatch breath ⱱ) and then at a fast tempo.

Natural Minor scale – ascending and descending 1 octave – first very slowly (with a snatch breath ⱱ) and then at a fast tempo.

Blues scale – 1 octave ascending and descending

Major arpeggio 1 octave ascending, with Major scale 1 octave descending

Intervals: **Major 2nd**   **Minor 3rd**   **Major 3rd**   **Perfect 4th**   **Perfect 5th**

Minor 6th   **Major 6th**   **Minor 7th**   **Major 7th**   **Octave**

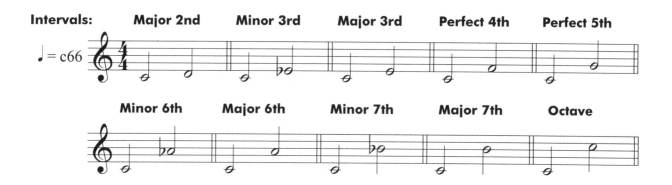

GRADE EIGHT

- The major and natural minor scales should be sung, to the range of a major 13th, ascending and descending slowly, and then (after a short pause) ascending and descending at a fast tempo.

- The chromatic scale should be sung ascending only – first slowly, and then (after a short pause) ascending again at a fast tempo.

- The minor arpeggio should be sung ascending only and then followed immediately (without a pause) by the natural minor scale descending. If desired, the arpeggio notes can be held longer than the scale notes.

- The major 9th and minor 9th arpeggios should be sung ascending and descending.

- Scales and arpeggios may be requested by the examiner to be sung either 'legato' (very smoothly) or 'articulated' (with a separate onset for each note).

- Intervals should be sung ascending only.

Major scale with range of major 13th – first very slowly (with a breath midway) and then at a fast tempo.

Chromatic scale – 1 octave ascending – first very slowly and then at a fast tempo

Minor arpeggio ascending with Natural Minor scale descending

Major 9th arpeggio – 1 octave ascending and descending

Minor 9th arpeggio – 1 octave ascending and descending

Intervals

 = c66

Performance

This section of the exam allows candidates to display their skills and talents using a 'free choice' of songs: musical styles and tastes are not imposed upon candidates. It has been deliberately designed as 'free and open' in order to allow candidates to select songs of their own choosing that are appropriate to their age, vocal range and abilities, and musical interests.

MAXIMUM MARKS for this section of the exam	
Grades 1 to 2:	70
Grades 3 to 8:	60

EXAM REQUIREMENTS

Depending upon grade, candidates should perform either 2 or 3 songs:

- For grades one, two and three, TWO songs, lasting no longer than 9 minutes in total, should be performed.

- For grades four and five, THREE songs, lasting no longer than 15 minutes in total, should be performed.

- For grades six, seven and eight, THREE songs, *plus* a verse and chorus (or any significant section) of one of the songs performed again *unaccompanied*, lasting no longer than 18 minutes in total, should be performed.

All timings should take account of gaps between songs.

The songs can be from any popular music style, such as pop, ballad, rock, soul, rock 'n' roll, jazz, r'n'b, reggae, funk, folk, metal, punk, grunge, indie, motown, country, blues, gospel, etc. The syllabus includes a large list of suggestions of popular songs and the typical grade at which each song might be presented, but candidates do not need to restrict their choice of songs to those presented on this list. However, at higher grades in particular, songs should be chosen that are technically sufficiently demanding to demonstrate the candidate's range of vocal abilities.

SONG CHOICE

- The choice of songs, and the keys and language in which they are sung, is at the candidate's discretion. The songs may include self-compositions, although no extra marks will be given for the 'composition' element.

- Whilst each song does not necessarily need to be from a different musical genre, the songs should be very carefully chosen so that they are sufficiently varied and contrasting – in order to demonstrate the candidate's vocal and expressive range, versatility and understanding of style, and the candidate's ability to deal with songs of different character, mood, tempo and period.

- Credit will be given for good repertoire selection that suits the singer's voice, whilst demonstrating 'versatility': for example, it is *highly recommended* that a slow song be balanced by an up-tempo song.

PROGRAMME

- A written programme of the songs that will be performed should be handed to the examiner at the start of the examination.

- From Grade 3 onwards, songs should also be verbally introduced including, at higher grades, some background information about each song (such as the name of the songwriter, the artist who made the song famous, the year in which it was a hit, etc.).

- A typed, or clearly written, lyric sheet for each song should be given to the examiner at the start of the exam – preferably for all grades, but as a requirement from Grade 6 onwards.

MEMORISATION

- Up to and including Grade 2 at least one song must be from memory, and credit will be given for additional performances from memory. From Grade 3 the whole programme should be from memory.

- Except for 'ad libs', and purely improvised sections, the lead melody line should be sung in full – with no sections omitted.

- Candidates, particularly at higher grades, are encouraged to include their own appropriate ad libs and other suitable improvisations.

BACKING (ACCOMPANIMENT)

- Candidates may bring a back-up musician (accompanist) or accompany themselves – but should be prepared to supply their own musical equipment (keyboard, guitar, etc.) if necessary or preferred. If candidates choose to play their own instrumental backing, they should ensure that they are able to perform this role without distracting from their vocal performance.

- The accompanist may only be present in the examination room during the section(s) in which he/she is playing.

- The quality of the accompanist's performance will not be examined, although candidates should satisfy themselves that the accompanist is adequately skilled to perform the role without distracting from the performance.

Alternatively, candidates may use backing tracks for accompaniment – providing these do NOT include lead vocals.

- Some exam centres may provide CD players (this should be checked with the local LCM representative at the time of entry), but all candidates should be prepared to bring their own suitable CD players, or minidisc players etc., when necessary or if preferred by them.

- From Grade 4, candidates must be able to set-up any accompaniment equipment quickly and efficiently and operate it unaided. Up to and including Grade Three, an adult may, with the examiner's consent, be present to operate the equipment.

- Backing tracks that are edited, and are thereby shorter than the original version of the song, may be used (for example, to omit purely instrumental sections) providing that no sections of the song where the lead melody would normally occur are omitted. In 'jazz standards' it is acceptable to omit the (introductory) verse where this is common practice.

- At all grades, it is the candidate's responsibility to ensure that the volume balance between the voice and the backing track is appropriate – so that the examiner can hear both clearly, especially the voice. The candidate may conduct one very short 'sound check' (approx. 30 seconds) before commencing the actual performances.

- Candidates should take care to choose backing tracks that are in a suitable key for their voice.

AMPLIFICATION

P.A. systems and microphones cannot be provided at most venues, therefore performances will normally be unamplified. However, candidates may bring a microphone (to be used unamplified) as a prop, if this makes them feel more comfortable.

- Where an examination centre provides an amplification system candidates can choose whether or not to use it, and if doing so may provide their own microphone if preferred.

- The examiner will not provide help in setting up or adjusting any amplification used: from Grade 4 candidates must be able to set-up and operate any amplification equipment used unaided and effectively (avoiding feedback, mic handling noises etc., and achieving a complementary tone). Up to and including Grade 3, an adult may, with the examiner's consent, be present to operate the equipment. The use of electronic effects (reverb, echo, etc.) should be minimal and should not interfere with the clarity of the vocals. No electronic pitch correction devices should be used.

EXAM TIPS

1   Whilst pop music may not be subject to the strict technical requirements of some other types of music, you are advised to develop a good singing technique as you progress through the grades. A vocal production that is obviously harmful to your voice will detract from your performance, no matter how good other aspects may be, and a candidate whose basic vocal production is obviously damaging their voice will see this reflected in the reduced mark awarded by the examiner.

2   Try to acquire a good feel for the styles you choose, as this will come over better than a technically perfect performance that is stilted. Pop music can be quite individualistic so don't be afraid to put yourself wholeheartedly into the performance of the song. Candidates should ensure that their rendition of each song is a committed 'performance', and candidates should not feel restricted by the examination environment. Whilst movements, gesticulation and emotive facial expressions are completely acceptable during the examination, be careful that such expressions do not get in the way of the song and interfere with the vocal performance: any movements should be a natural extension of the performance and not an adjunct.

3   Although awareness of style is important, examiners are not looking for 'vocal impersonators'. Candidates, particularly those with changing or developing voices, may change the key of a song to make it more suitable for their voice. Singing a song in the original key, where this creates a more challenging range, may move a song to a higher grade than that shown in the Sample Song List in the syllabus, but candidates should take care not to attempt songs in keys that may cause them to strain their voices unduly. Whilst the syllabus does not stipulate the original key, candidates should be aware that choosing an inappropriate key can result in a loss of style and tone and may inhibit the necessary vitality and excitement of the song.

4   Make sure that you have thoroughly learned the lyrics for songs that are required to be from memory. Any lapses of memory should be disguised: try not to be disconcerted by any such slips, and always avoid the temptation to stop or re-take a line.

5   In the higher grades (6-8) technical ability becomes increasingly important and the examiner will expect an appropriate vocal technique to underpin the chosen songs. A good teacher, a careful selection of vocal exercises and regular practice will be invaluable.

6   The quality of the performance will be the main factor in deciding the grade level of a particular song. However, the syllabus outlines the technical information that should be taken into consideration as general guidelines when assessing the technical level and grade of a song. The syllabus is also very comprehensive regarding the assessment criteria for this section of the exam and you are advised to read this thoroughly. However, the list overleaf shows the main criteria by which performances are judged across the grades. You should try to consider all of these aspects when preparing for the exam.

- Accuracy of melody
- Ability to complete the performance
- Security of rhythm, timing, and pulse
- Breath control, phrasing and sustain
- Accurate or intentionally relaxed intonation
- Tonal quality
- Technical control
- Expression
- Variety and suitability of programme
- Memory – ability to memorise and/or to cope with minor memory lapses if they occur
- Communication and interpretation
- Stylistically appropriate vocal production
- Confidence of the performance
- Dynamics
- Articulation
- Diction
- Presentation
- Accuracy of lyrics
- Rehearsed familiarity with the accompaniment and evidence of careful preparation
- Sensitivity and portrayal of the emotion of the song
- Ability to maintain vocal control during movement or dance
- Evidence of commitment to the performance and enthusiasm for the genre
- A technique that is at least sufficiently stress-free for the vocal mechanism to survive repeated performances
- Adequate vocal range and well-managed register changes

Musical knowledge

THIS SECTION OF THE EXAM OCCURS ONLY FROM GRADE THREE ONWARDS

This section of the exam is designed to ensure that candidates have a secure understanding of some of the most relevant aspects of the theory and musical language of popular music. A good understanding of these topics will enable vocalists to communicate freely and effectively with other musicians.

By studying for this section of the exam candidates will gain knowledge about:

- musical terms and signs
- time signatures and rhythm notation
- scales, keys, intervals, chords/arpeggios
- transposing chord progressions

These topics have been chosen as they are considered the most useful for singers in relation to practical music-making.

All the information required for this section of the exam, and more, is contained within the LCM Popular Music Theory handbooks, and it is *highly recommended* that all candidates study not only the relevant theory handbook for the equivalent grade, but also the preceding handbooks in the series.

The LCM Popular Music Theory handbooks are available from good music/book stores, or by mail order from Registry Publications (020 8665 7666) or at www.BooksForMusic.com

MAXIMUM MARKS for this section of the exam	
Grades 3 to 8	10

EXEMPTIONS FROM THIS SECTION OF THE EXAM

Candidates who have obtained a pass in the same or higher grade of the LCM Popular Music Theory exams have the option not be tested on this section of the examination. Instead they may choose to be credited up to full marks for this section of examination (depending upon the result of their popular music theory examination). Candidates choosing this option must show a copy of their popular music theory report or certificate to the examiner at the start of the examination.

- Candidates who have an Honours pass in popular music theory, at the same or higher grade, will be awarded 10 marks for this section of the exam.
- Candidates who have a Merit pass in popular music theory, at the same or higher grade, will be awarded 8 marks for this section of the exam.
- Candidates who have a Pass in popular music theory, at the same or higher grade, will be awarded 7 marks for this section of the exam.

EXAM CONTENT

Candidates who have not passed the popular music theory exam, and candidates not choosing the option described above, will be asked a selection of questions, appropriate to the grade, as outlined on the following pages.

Whilst the questions asked will generally be related to the topics set for Section One (Technical Knowledge) of this exam, they will also cover a broader area of related subjects.

The questions will all be asked verbally by the examiner and, in order to gain high marks, prompt responses will be expected – rather than candidates 'working out' answers.

Normally about three questions will be asked, with each correct response being awarded a maximum of 3 marks, and an extra mark being available for particularly clear and prompt responses.

SPECIMEN QUESTIONS

The specimen questions that follow are supplied in order to provide a general guideline to, and some examples of, the type of questions that may be asked at each grade, however the list of questions shown is neither exclusive nor exhaustive. Specimen answers are provided to give some indication of the depth and detail required in responses, however it is stressed that the answers are samples.

TERMINOLOGY

Providing there is a consistent approach, candidates may use either contemporary or traditional musical terminology when giving responses; for example, the terms 'crotchet' and 'quarter note' have the same meaning, and either term may be used. In the specimen questions and answers below, the traditional term is shown in brackets after the contemporary term.

Care should be taken to use the correct 'enharmonic spelling' when responding to questions. For example, the note (and any chord built on that note) on the 7th degree of the G major scale should be called F# rather than G♭, even though both notes are of equivalent pitch.

GRADE THREE

At this grade candidates should have a *practical* understanding of the following:

- ■ ¼ time signature
- ■ basic repeat markings
- ■ basic dynamic markings

Typical questions, and specimen answers, might be:

Q1. What does ¼ time mean?

A1. Four quarter note (crotchet) beats in each bar.

Q2. Give a one bar 'count-in' at a slow/medium/fast tempo in ¼ time.

A2. <u>One</u>, Two, Three, Four. (The candidate's count should be at a very even tempo, with the beats well-defined and the first beat accented).

For the following types of questions, the candidate will be shown a short musical score in standard notation, similar in style to that shown below.

Q3. What do the two vertical dots at the end of bar 2 indicate?

A3. These are repeat dots. As there are no previous (right facing) repeat dots, the performer should repeat from the beginning up until this point before continuing – i.e. bars 1 and 2 should be repeated.

Q4. What do the two vertical dots at the end of bar 4 indicate?

A4. These are repeat dots. The performer should repeat from the previous (right facing) repeat dots up until this point before continuing – i.e. bars 3 and 4 should be repeated.

Q5. What does the *mf* under bar 1 mean?

A5. This is a dynamic marking meaning to sing at a moderately loud volume (moderately strong).

Q6. What does the *p* under bar 3 mean?

A6. This is a dynamic marking meaning to sing softly.

Q7. What does the *f* under bar 5 mean?

A7. This is a dynamic marking meaning to sing strongly (at a loud volume).

GRADE FOUR

At this grade candidates should have a *practical* understanding of the following:

- $\frac{3}{4}$ and $\frac{4}{4}$ time signatures
- repeat markings
- dynamic markings

Typical questions, and specimen answers, might be:

Q1.   Explain the difference between $\frac{3}{4}$ and $\frac{4}{4}$ time.

A1. $\frac{4}{4}$ time equates to four quarter note (crotchet) beats per bar, whereas $\frac{3}{4}$ time has three quarter note (crotchet) beats per bar.

Q2.   Give a two bar 'count-in' at a slow/medium/fast tempo in $\frac{3}{4}$ time.

A2.   <u>One</u>, Two, Three, <u>One</u>, Two, Three. (The candidate's count should be at a very even tempo, with the beats well-defined and the first beat of each bar accented).

For the following types of questions, the candidate will be shown a short musical score in standard notation, similar in style to that shown below.

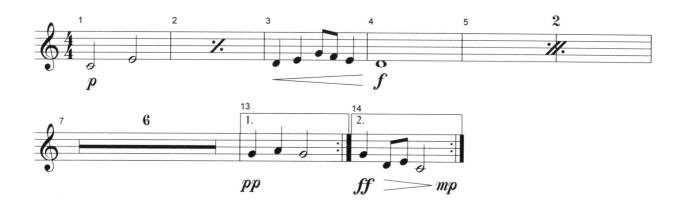

Q3.   What does the symbol in bar 2 indicate?

A3.   Repeat the previous bar.

Q4. What does the symbol across bars 5 and 6 indicate?

A4. Repeat the previous two bars.

Q5. What does the symbol in bar 7 indicate?

A5. Rest for six bars.

Q6. What do the numbers above bars 13 and 14 indicate?

A6. These are first and second time endings: the first time through you should include bar 13, but this bar should be omitted and replaced with bar 14 the second time round.

Q7. What does the sign ——————— under bar 3 indicate?

A7. Gradually increase in volume (crescendo).

Q8. What does the *pp* under bar 13 mean?

A8. This is a dynamic marking meaning to sing very softly.

Q9. What does the *ff* under bar 14 mean?

A9. This is a dynamic marking meaning to sing very strongly.

Q10. What does the sign ——————— towards the end of bar 14 indicate?

A10. Gradually decrease in volume (decrescendo).

GRADE FIVE

At this grade candidates should have a *practical* understanding of the following:

- ■ $\frac{3}{4}$ $\frac{4}{4}$ and $\frac{6}{8}$ time signatures
- ■ repeat markings
- ■ key signatures (up to 2 sharps or 2 flats)

Typical questions, and specimen answers, might be:

Q1. Explain in practical terms what the time signature $\frac{6}{8}$ refers to.

A1. Two dotted quarter note (dotted crotchet) beats per bar – equivalent to six eighth notes (quavers) per bar.

Q2. Give a two bar 'count-in' at a slow/medium/fast tempo in $\frac{6}{8}$ time.

A2. <u>ONE</u> Two Three TWO Two Three, <u>ONE</u> Two Three TWO Two Three. (Candidates can count ONE Two Three FOUR Five Six for each bar if preferred. The candidate's count should be at a very even tempo, with the two main beats well-defined and the first beat of each bar accented).

For the following types of questions, the candidate will be shown one or more short musical scores in standard notation, similar in style to those shown below.

Example 1

Example 2

Example 3

Example 4

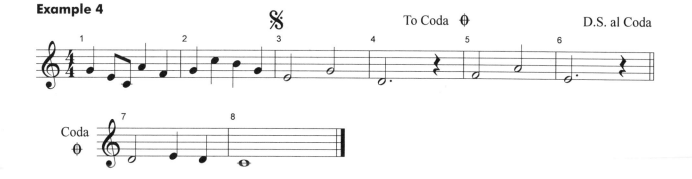

Q3. What does the marking *D.C. al Fine* indicate?

A3. Repeat from the beginning up until the point marked 'Fine' – i.e. in Example 1 repeat from bar 1 to the end of bar 6.

Q4. What does the marking *D.S. al Fine* indicate?

A4. Repeat from the sign ℅ up until the point marked 'Fine' – i.e. in Example 2 repeat from bar 3 to the end of bar 6.

Q5. What does the marking *D.C. al Coda* indicate?

A5. Repeat from the beginning up until the first coda sign ⊕ and then go straight to the Coda – i.e. in Example 3 repeat from bar 1 to the end of bar 2, and then go to bar 5.

Q6. What does the marking *D.S. al Coda* indicate?

A6. Repeat from the sign ℅ up until the first coda sign ⊕ and then go straight to the Coda – i.e. in Example 4 repeat from bar 3 to the end of bar 4, and then go to bar 7.

Q7. Which minor key signature is represented by 1 sharp (as in Example i below)?

A7. E minor

Q8. Which major key signature is represented by 2 sharps (as in Example ii)?

A8. D major

Q9. Which minor key signature is represented by 1 flat (as in Example iii)?

A9. D minor

Q10. Which major key signature is represented by 2 flats (as in Example iv)?

A10. B♭ major

(i)   **(ii)**   **(iii)**   **(iv)**

GRADE SIX

At this grade, candidates should have a practical understanding of the following:

- $\frac{3}{4}$ $\frac{4}{4}$ $\frac{6}{8}$ and $\frac{12}{8}$ time signatures
- basic note values – ranging from a whole note (semibreve) to an eighth note (quaver)
- key signatures (up to 3 sharps or 3 flats)
- construction and interval spellings of major and natural minor scales

Q1. Explain in practical terms what the time signature $\frac{12}{8}$ refers to.

A1. Four dotted quarter note (dotted crotchet) beats per bar – equivalent to twelve eighth notes (quavers) per bar.

Q2. Give a one bar 'count-in' at a slow/medium/fast tempo in $\frac{12}{8}$ time.

A2. ONE Two Three TWO Two Three THREE Two Three FOUR Two Three (Candidates can count ONE Two Three FOUR Five Six SEVEN Eight Nine TEN Eleven Twelve, or ONE, TWO, THREE, FOUR, for each bar if preferred. The candidate's count should be at a very even tempo, with the four main beats accented).

Q3. How many quarter notes (crotchets) are equivalent to a whole note (semibreve)?

A3. Four

Q4. How many eighth notes (quavers) are equivalent to a half note (minim)?

A4. Four

Q5. In $\frac{4}{4}$ time, how many beats does a half note (minim) last for?

A5. Two

Q6. How many eighth notes (quavers) can appear in a bar of $\frac{3}{4}$ time?

A6. Six

Q7. How many sharps or flats appear in the key signature for E♭ major?

A7. Three

Q8. Which minor key signature has the same key signature as A major?

A8. F# minor

Q9. Describe the construction of the major scale in terms of whole tones and semitones (or whole steps and half steps)

A9. Tone Tone Semitone Tone Tone Tone Semitone (Whole Whole Half Whole Whole Whole Half)

Q10. What is the interval spelling of the natural minor scale?

A10. 1 2 ♭3 4 5 ♭6 ♭7 8

GRADE SEVEN

At this grade candidates should have a practical understanding of the following:

- basic note values – ranging from a whole note (semibreve) to a 16th note (semiquaver)

- key signatures (up to 4 sharps or 4 flats)

- construction and interval spellings of major and minor chords; major 7th, minor 7th and dominant 7th chords

- basic transposition: transposing a short major key chord progression either up or down a whole step (whole tone) or a half step (semitone) within a range of keys up to 4 sharps or 4 flats

Q1. How many 16th notes (semiquavers) are equivalent to a quarter note (crotchet)?

A1. Four

Q2. How many 16th notes (semiquavers) can occur in a bar of $\frac{6}{8}$ time?

A2. 12

Q3. Which major key has a key signature of four sharps?

A3. E major

Q4. Which minor key has a key signature of four flats?

A4. F minor

Q5. Which intervals of the major scale make up the major chord/arpeggio?

A5. 1st, 3rd and 5th

Q6. Which intervals of the major scale make up the major 7th chord/arpeggio?

A6. 1st, 3rd, 5th and 7th

Q7. What is the interval spelling for a minor arpeggio?

A7. 1, ♭3, 5

Q8. What is the correct interval spelling for a minor 7th arpeggio?

A8. 1, ♭3, 5, ♭7

Q9. What is the interval spelling for a dominant 7th arpeggio?

A9. 1, 3, 5, ♭7

Q10. Transpose the following chord progression from the key of C major into the key of D major: C Dm F G

A10. D Em G A

Q11. Transpose the following chord progression from the key of G major into the key of F major: G C Em D

A11. F B♭ Dm C

GRADE EIGHT

At this grade, candidates should have a *practical* understanding of the following:

- note values – ranging from a whole note (semibreve) to a 16th note (semiquaver), and including dotted notes
- all key signatures
- construction and interval spellings of: blues scale; major 9th and minor 9th chords
- transposition: transposing a short major or minor key chord progression into any near or related key

Q1. How many quarter notes (crotchets) are equivalent to a dotted half note (dotted minim)?

A1. Three

Q2. How many eighth notes (quavers) are equivalent to a dotted quarter note (dotted crotchet)?

A2. Three

Q3. Which major key has a key signature of six sharps?

A3. F# major

Q4. Which minor key has a key signature of five flats?

A4. B♭ minor

Q5. What is the interval spelling of the blues scale?

A5. 1 ♭3 4 ♭5 (or #4) 5 ♭7 8

Q6. Which intervals of the major scale make-up the major 9th chord/arpeggio?

A6. 1st, 3rd, 5th, 7th and 9th

Q7. What is the correct interval spelling for a minor 9th arpeggio?

A7. 1, ♭3, 5, ♭7, 9

Q8. Transpose the following chord progression from the key of C major into the key of G major: C F Am G

A8. G C Em D

Q9. Transpose the following chord progression from the key of E major into the key of A major: E F#m B A

A9. A Bm E D

Q10. Transpose the following chord progression from the key of C minor into the key of G minor: Cm Fm A♭ B♭

A10. Gm Cm E♭ F

Q11. Transpose the following chord progression from the key of G major into the key of G♭ major: G C Am D

A11. G♭ C♭ A♭m D♭

Aural Awareness

This section of the exam is designed to ensure that candidates develop a good level of aural awareness. Studying aural awareness will help vocalists to:

- hear, recognise and reproduce rhythms, melodic phrases and harmony lines

- recognise intervals, chords and chord changes

- keep time and recognise time signatures

MAXIMUM MARKS for this section of the exam	
Grades 1 to 5:	15
Grades 6 to 8:	10

The musical examples that follow are supplied in order to provide a clear indication of the *type* and *range* of tests that will be given in each grade. The examiner may play the tests on piano, keyboard or guitar, at the examiner's discretion. When playing chords the examiner will play block (non-arpeggiated) chords, using any standard 'root position' voicing (e.g. some notes may be doubled) but *excluding* inversions.

GRADE ONE

REPETITION OF RHYTHM GRADE ONE

The examiner will twice play (on a single note) a two bar rhythm in $\frac{4}{4}$ time which will consist of a mixture of half notes (minims), quarter notes (crotchets) and eighth notes (quavers). The candidate should then reproduce this rhythm by clapping. The test will be given at a moderately quick tempo ($\quarternote$ = c120).

KEEPING TIME GRADE ONE

The examiner will twice play a four bar phrase in $\frac{4}{4}$ time. During the second playing the candidate should clap the main pulse, accenting the first beat of each bar.

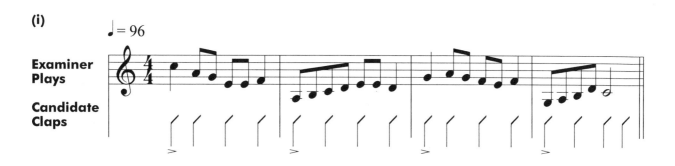

(ii)

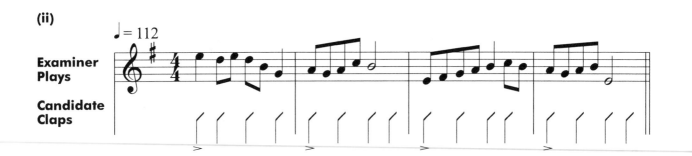

REPETITION OF A MELODIC PHRASE GRADE ONE

The examiner will play a one bar phrase in $\frac{4}{4}$ time consisting of adjacent notes taken from the one octave major scale, and beginning with the keynote. The phrase will consist of quarter notes (crotchets) and eighth notes (quavers). The examiner will select a suitable key and octave according to the age and gender of the candidate.

The examiner will play the phrase twice, and the candidate will then be expected to sing back the phrase. The test will be given at a fairly slow tempo ($\downarrow$ = c72).

Ex. 1

Ex. 2

Ex. 3

Ex. 4

RECOGNITION OF INTERVALS GRADE ONE

Whilst the candidate looks away, the examiner will play the root note of a major arpeggio followed by another note from the arpeggio. The candidate will then be asked to identify the second note by interval number. The interval may be repeated at the candidate's request.

(Major) 3rd   (Perfect) 5th   Octave

RECOGNITION OF CHORDS GRADE ONE

Whilst the candidate looks away, the examiner will play a few bars of music containing either all major or all minor chords. The candidate will then be asked to identify which type of chord was used.

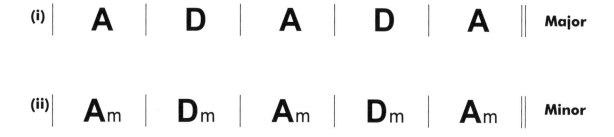

(i) | A | D | A | D | A ‖ Major

(ii) | Am | Dm | Am | Dm | Am ‖ Minor

GRADE TWO

REPETITION OF RHYTHM GRADE TWO

The examiner will twice play (on a single note) a four bar rhythm in either $\frac{3}{4}$ or $\frac{4}{4}$ time which will consist of a mixture of half notes (minims), quarter notes (crotchets) and eighth notes (quavers) – except for the final bar which will contain only one long note. The candidate should then reproduce this rhythm by clapping. Note that the first and third bars will be identical. The test will be given at a moderate tempo ($\downarrow$ = c116).

KEEPING TIME GRADE TWO

The examiner will twice play a four bar phrase in either $\frac{3}{4}$ or $\frac{4}{4}$ time. During the second playing the candidate should clap the main pulse, accenting the first beat of each bar.

(i)

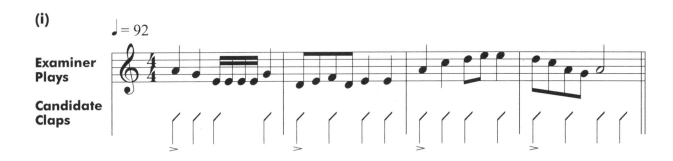

(ii)

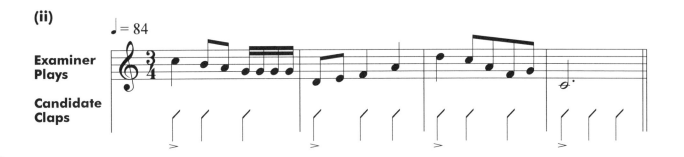

REPETITION OF A MELODIC PHRASE GRADE TWO

The examiner will play a one bar phrase in ⁴⁄₄ time consisting of notes taken from the one octave major scale, and beginning with the keynote. The phrase will consist of quarter notes (crotchets) and eighth notes (quavers). The examiner will select a suitable key and octave according to the age and gender of the candidate.

The examiner will play the phrase twice, and the candidate will then be expected to sing back the phrase. The test will be given at a fairly slow tempo (♩ = c72).

RECOGNITION OF INTERVALS GRADE TWO

Whilst the candidate looks away, the examiner will play the keynote of a major scale, followed by another note taken from the first five degrees of the major scale. The candidate will then be asked to identify the second note by interval number. The interval may be repeated at the candidate's request.

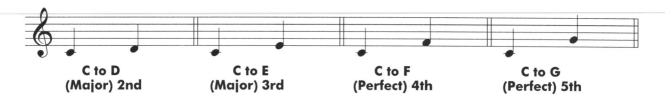

| C to D | C to E | C to F | C to G |
| (Major) 2nd | (Major) 3rd | (Perfect) 4th | (Perfect) 5th |

RECOGNITION OF CHORDS GRADE TWO

Whilst the candidate looks away, the examiner will play either a single major chord followed by a minor chord, or a single minor chord followed by a major chord. The candidate will then be asked to identify the order of the chord types.

$$C - A_m \quad = \quad \text{major/minor}$$

$$E_m - C \quad = \quad \text{minor/major}$$

GRADE THREE

REPETITION OF RHYTHM GRADE THREE

The examiner will twice play (on a single note) a four bar rhythm in either $\frac{3}{4}$, $\frac{6}{8}$ or $\frac{4}{4}$ time which will consist of a mixture of half notes (minims), dotted quarter notes (dotted crotchets), quarter notes (crotchets) and eighth notes (quavers) – except for the final bar which will contain only one long note. The candidate should then reproduce this rhythm by clapping. Note that the first and third bars will be identical.

KEEPING TIME GRADE THREE

The examiner will twice play a four bar phrase in either $\frac{3}{4}$, $\frac{6}{8}$ or $\frac{4}{4}$ time. During the second playing the candidate should clap the main pulse, accenting the first beat of each bar.

(ii)

(iii)

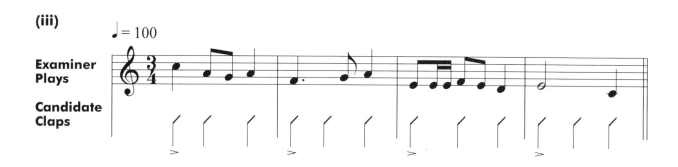

REPETITION OF A MELODIC PHRASE GRADE THREE

The examiner will play a one bar phrase in ¾ time consisting of notes taken from the one octave major scale, and beginning with either the keynote or the fifth degree of the scale. The phrase will consist of quarter notes (crotchets) and eighth notes (quavers). The examiner will select a suitable key and octave according to the age and gender of the candidate.

The examiner will play the phrase twice, the candidate will then be expected to sing the phrase. The test will be given at a slow to moderate tempo (♩ = c80).

RECOGNITION OF INTERVALS GRADE THREE

Whilst the candidate looks away, the examiner will play the keynote of a major scale, followed by another note taken from within one octave of the major scale. The candidate will then be asked to identify the second note by interval number. The interval may be repeated at the candidate's request.

RECOGNITION OF CHORDS GRADE THREE

Whilst the candidate looks away, the examiner will twice play either a major chord or a minor chord. The candidate will then be asked to identify whether the chord was major or minor.

GRADE FOUR

REPETITION OF RHYTHM GRADE FOUR

The examiner will twice play (on a single note) a four bar rhythm in either $\frac{3}{4}$, $\frac{6}{8}$ or $\frac{4}{4}$ time which will consist of a mixture of dotted quarter notes (dotted crotchets), quarter notes (crotchets), eighth notes (quavers) and sixteenth notes (semiquavers) – except for the last bar, which will contain only one long note. The candidate should then reproduce this rhythm by clapping. Note that the first and third bars will be identical.

KEEPING TIME & RECOGNISING TIME SIGNATURE GRADE FOUR

The examiner will twice play a four bar phrase in either $\frac{3}{4}$, $\frac{6}{8}$ or $\frac{4}{4}$ time. After the first playing the candidate should identify the time signature. During the second playing the candidate should clap the main pulse, accenting the first beat of each bar.

(ii)

Examiner Plays

Candidate Claps

(iii)

Examiner Plays

Candidate Claps

REPETITION OF A MELODIC PHRASE GRADE FOUR

The examiner will play a two bar phrase in either $\frac{6}{8}$ or $\frac{4}{4}$ time, consisting of notes taken from the one octave major scale and starting from any degree of the scale. The phrase will contain no note value shorter than an eighth note (quaver).

The examiner will select a suitable key and octave according to the age and gender of the candidate.

The examiner will play the phrase twice, and the candidate will then be expected to sing back the phrase. The test will be given at a slow to moderate tempo: ($\quad$ = c84, $\quad$ = c54).

RECOGNITION OF INTERVALS GRADE FOUR

Whilst the candidate looks away, the examiner will play an interval of a 3rd or a 7th in any key – sounding the notes separately. The candidate will then be asked to identify whether the interval was major or minor. For example:

C to E♭ (minor 3rd)   C to E (major 3rd)   C to B♭ (minor 7th)   C to B (major 7th)

The interval may be repeated at the candidate's request.

RECOGNITION OF CHORDS GRADE FOUR

Whilst the candidate looks away, the examiner will twice play either a major 7th, minor 7th or dominant 7th chord. The candidate will then be asked to identify the type of chord that was played.

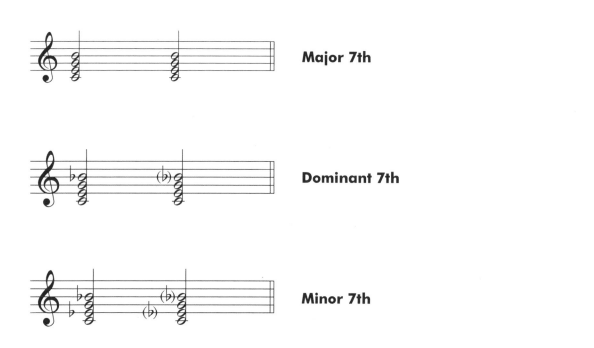

Major 7th

Dominant 7th

Minor 7th

GRADE FIVE

REPETITION OF RHYTHM GRADE FIVE

The examiner will twice play (on a single note) a four bar rhythm in either ¾, ⁶⁄₈ or ⁴⁄₄ time which will contain no note value shorter than a sixteenth note (semiquaver). The candidate should then reproduce this rhythm by clapping.

Note that the third bar will be a *variation* of the first bar, whilst the fourth bar will contain one long note.

KEEPING TIME & RECOGNISING TIME SIGNATURE GRADE FIVE

The examiner will twice play a four bar melody in either ¾, ⁶⁄₈ or ⁴⁄₄ time. The melody will not begin on the first beat of the bar. After the first playing the candidate should identify the time signature. During the second playing the candidate should clap the main pulse, accenting the first beat of each bar.

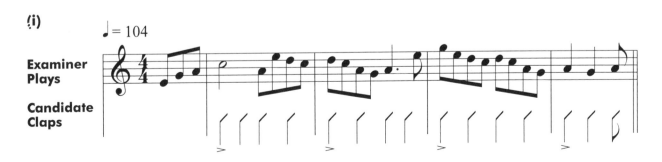

(ii)

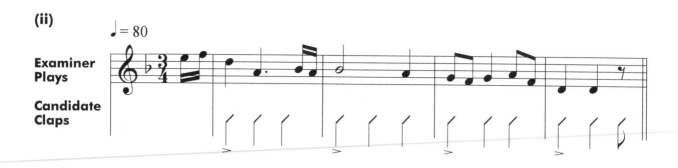

(iii)

REPETITION OF A MELODIC PHRASE GRADE FIVE

The examiner will play a four bar phrase in either ⅜ or ¼ time, consisting of notes taken from the one octave major scale and starting from any degree of the scale. The phrase will contain no note value shorter than an eighth note (quaver). The third bar will be a repeat of the first bar.

The examiner will select a suitable key and octave according to the age and gender of the candidate.

The examiner will play the phrase twice, and the candidate will then be expected to sing back the phrase.

RECOGNITION OF INTERVALS GRADE FIVE

Whilst the candidate looks away, the examiner will play a one octave scale. The candidate will then be asked to identify whether the scale was major or minor.

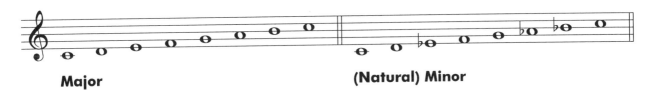

Major   **(Natural) Minor**

RECOGNITION OF CHORDS GRADE FIVE

Whilst the candidate looks away, the examiner will play a short chord progression in either a major or minor key. The candidate will then be asked to identify whether the key was major or minor.

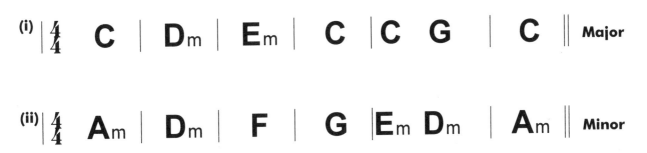

(i) | 4/4 | C | Dm | Em | C | C G | C || Major

(ii) | 4/4 | Am | Dm | F | G | Em Dm | Am || Minor

GRADE SIX

REPETITION OF RHYTHM GRADE SIX

The examiner will twice play (on a single note) a 4 bar rhythm, in either ¾, ⁶⁄₈ or ⁴⁄₄ time, which will contain no note value shorter than a sixteenth note (semiquaver). The candidate should then reproduce this rhythm by clapping.

Note that the third bar will be a repeat of the first bar, whilst the fourth bar will be a variation of the second bar.

KEEPING TIME & RECOGNISING TIME SIGNATURE GRADE SIX

The examiner will twice play a four bar melody in either ¾, ⁶⁄₈, ¹²⁄₈ or ⁴⁄₄ time. The melody will not begin on the first beat of the bar. After the first playing the candidate should identify the time signature. During the second playing the candidate should clap the main pulse, accenting the first beat of each bar.

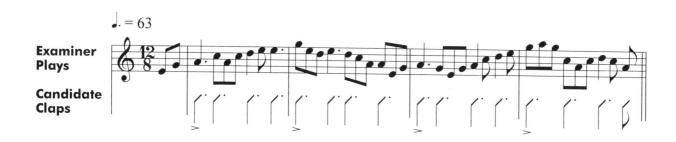

HARMONISATION OF A MELODIC PHRASE GRADE SIX

This test is designed to assess the candidate's ability to create a harmony line by ear. The candidate will need to find a harmony line, above or below the original phrase, that is appropriate to the melody and the candidate's voice. At this grade, no more than a simple parallel harmony, such as a harmony line based a 3rd above, will be expected.

The examiner will play the tonic chord followed by a two bar phrase in either ⁴⁄₄ or ⁶⁄₈. The phrase will contain no note value shorter than an eighth note. The phrase will be in a major key and will contain no interval greater than a major 3rd. The notation will not be shown to the candidate.

The examiner will play the phrase again, and ask the candidate to prepare a harmony line – this can be done out loud (or in an 'undervoice' if preferred) as the examiner plays. The examiner will then play the phrase a further two times to allow the candidate to refine the harmony line. The examiner will then play the melody a final time and ask the candidate to join in singing the finished harmony line. The examiner will assess only this final performance: the preparatory attempts will not influence the marks awarded.

Here are some examples of the *type* of phrase which may be played.

RECOGNITION OF INTERVALS GRADE SIX

The candidate will be asked to identify any diatonic interval from the major scale, up to and including the major 9th, plus the diminished 5th and augmented 5th. Whilst the candidate looks away, the examiner will play the keynote followed by another note. The candidate will then be asked to identify the second note by interval number. The interval may be repeated at the candidate's request. Here is an example in the key of A major.

RECOGNITION OF CADENCES GRADE SIX

Whilst the candidate looks away, the examiner will play a short chord progression in a major key ending with either a perfect (V–I) or plagal (IV–I) cadence. The candidate will then be asked to identify the cadence.

(A perfect cadence is a movement from the V (dominant) chord to the I (tonic) chord. A plagal cadence is a movement from the IV (sub-dominant) chord to the I (tonic) chord.)

(i) | $\frac{4}{4}$ | C | Am | Dm | G C ‖ **Perfect (V–I) cadence**

(ii) | $\frac{4}{4}$ | C | Em | G | F C ‖ **Plagal (IV–I) cadence**

GRADE SEVEN

REPETITION OF RHYTHM GRADE SEVEN

The examiner will twice play (on a single note) a four bar rhythm, in either ¾, ⅜ or ⁴⁄₄ time. The candidate should then reproduce this rhythm by clapping.

Note that the third bar will be a repeat of the first bar, whilst the fourth bar will be a variation of the second bar.

The rhythm will contain no note value shorter than a sixteenth note (semiquaver), but may include triplets.

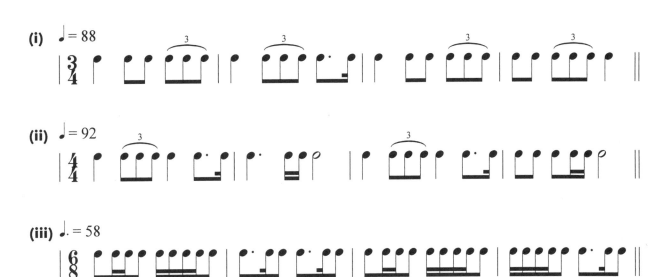

KEEPING TIME & RECOGNISING TIME SIGNATURE GRADE SEVEN

The examiner will twice play a four bar melody in either ¾, ⅜, ¹²⁄₈ or ⁴⁄₄ time. The melody will not begin on the first beat of the bar, and may include triplets. After the first playing the candidate should identify the time signature. During the second playing the candidate should clap the main pulse, accenting the first beat of each bar.

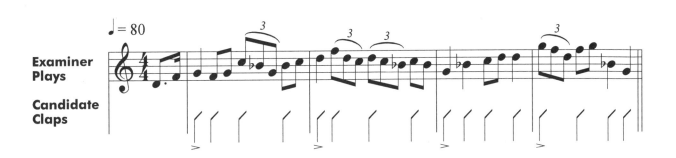

HARMONISATION OF A MELODIC PHRASE GRADE SEVEN

This test is designed to assess the candidate's ability to create a harmony line by ear. The candidate will need to find a harmony line, above or below the original phrase, that is appropriate to the melody and the candidate's voice. At this grade, a simple parallel harmony, such as a harmony line based a 3rd or 6th above or below, will be acceptable; although the examiner will give credit for other interesting harmonies that work well.

The examiner will play the tonic chord followed by a two bar phrase in either $\frac{4}{4}$ or $\frac{6}{8}$. The phrase will contain no note value shorter than a 16th note, and may include tied notes. The phrase will be in a major key and will contain no interval greater than a perfect 5th. The notation will not be shown to the candidate.

The examiner will play the phrase again, and ask the candidate to prepare a harmony line – this can be done out loud (or in an 'undervoice' if preferred) as the examiner plays. The examiner will then play the phrase a further two times to allow the candidate to refine the harmony line. The examiner will then play the melody a final time and ask the candidate to join in singing the finished harmony line. The examiner will assess only this final performance: the preparatory attempts will not influence the marks awarded.

Here are some examples of the *type* of phrase which may be played.

RECOGNITION OF INTERVALS GRADE SEVEN

The candidate will be asked to identify any interval ranging from a minor 2nd up to and including an augmented 9th. Whilst the candidate looks away, the examiner will play the keynote followed by another note. The candidate will then be asked to identify the second note by interval number. The interval may be repeated at the candidate's request. Here is an example with a keynote of G.

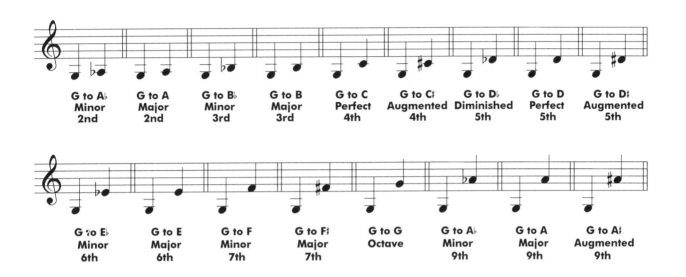

RECOGNITION OF CADENCES GRADE SEVEN

Whilst the candidate looks away, the examiner will play a short chord progression in a major key ending with either a perfect, plagal, imperfect or interrupted cadence. The candidate will then be asked to identify the type of cadence that the progression ends with.

Here are some examples in the key of C major:

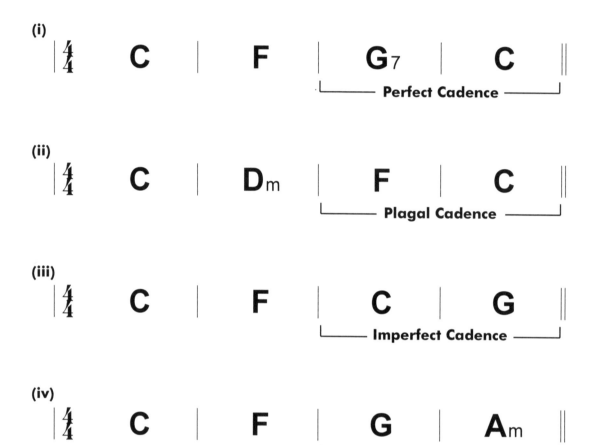

(i)	Perfect Cadence	– this is a movement from the V (dominant) chord to the I (tonic) chord.
(ii)	Plagal Cadence	– this is a movement from the IV (sub-dominant) chord to the I (tonic) chord.
(iii)	Imperfect Cadence	– this is a movement from the I (tonic) chord to the V (dominant) chord.
(iv)	Interrupted Cadence	– this is a movement from the V (dominant) chord to a chord other than the I (tonic) chord. Normally the movement is to the VIm chord.

GRADE EIGHT

REPETITION OF RHYTHM GRADE EIGHT

The examiner will twice play (on a single note) a four bar rhythm, in either ¾, ⁶⁄₈, ⁴⁄₄ or ⁵⁄₄ time. The candidate should then reproduce this rhythm by clapping.

Note that either the third bar will be a repeat of the first bar, or the fourth bar will be a repeat of the second bar.

The rhythm will contain no note value shorter than a sixteenth note (semiquaver), but may include triplets and tied notes.

(i) ♩ = 84

(ii) ♩ = 92

(iii) ♩. = 63

KEEPING TIME & RECOGNISING TIME SIGNATURE GRADE EIGHT

The examiner will twice play a four bar melody in either ¾, ⁶⁄₈, ¹²⁄₈, ⁴⁄₄ or ⁵⁄₄ time. The melody may begin on any beat of the bar, and may include triplets and tied notes.

After the first playing the candidate should identify the time signature. During the second playing the candidate should clap the main pulse, accenting the first beat of each bar.

Some examples are shown overleaf.

(i)

(ii)

HARMONISATION OF A MELODIC PHRASE GRADE EIGHT

This test is designed to assess the candidate's ability to create a harmony line by ear. The candidate will need to find a harmony line, above or below the original phrase, that is appropriate to the melody and the candidate's voice. At this grade, as well as standard parallel harmonies, such as a harmony line based a 3rd or 6th above or below, the examiner will give extra credit for more interesting harmonies that work well.

The examiner will play the tonic chord followed by a two bar phrase in either $\frac{4}{4}$ or $\frac{6}{8}$. The phrase will contain no note value shorter than a 16th note, and may include tied notes. The phrase may be in either a major or minor key, and will contain no interval greater than a major 6th. The notation will not be shown to the candidate.

The examiner will play the phrase again, and ask the candidate to prepare a harmony line – this can be done out loud (or in an 'undervoice' if preferred) as the examiner plays. The examiner will then play the phrase a further two times to allow the candidate to refine the harmony line. The examiner will then play the melody a final time and ask the candidate to join in singing the finished harmony line. The examiner will assess only this final performance: the preparatory attempts will not influence the marks awarded.

Some examples of the *type* of phrase which may be played are shown on the following page.

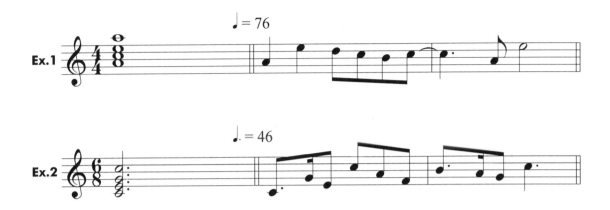

RECOGNITION OF INTERVALS GRADE EIGHT

The candidate will be asked to identify any interval ranging from a minor 2nd up to and including a perfect 11th, plus a major 13th. Whilst the candidate looks away, the examiner will play the keynote followed by another note. The candidate will then be asked to identify the second note by interval number. The interval may be repeated at the candidate's request. Here is an example with a keynote of C.

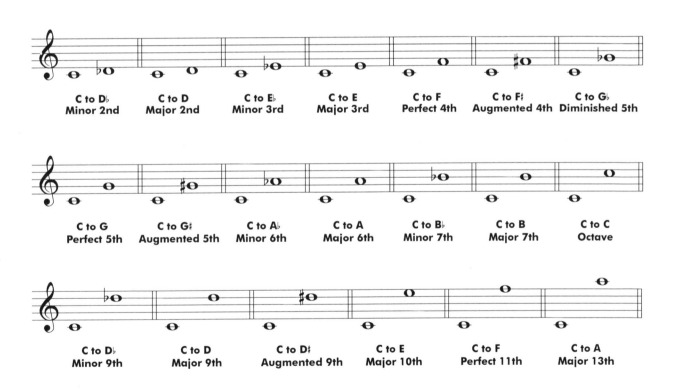

RECOGNITION OF CADENCES GRADE EIGHT

Whilst the candidate looks away, the examiner will play a short chord progression in a major key – including two cadences: either perfect (V–I), plagal (IV–I), imperfect (I–V) or interrupted (V–VIm). The candidate will then be asked to identify the types of cadence that were included in the progression.

Here are two examples in the key of G major:

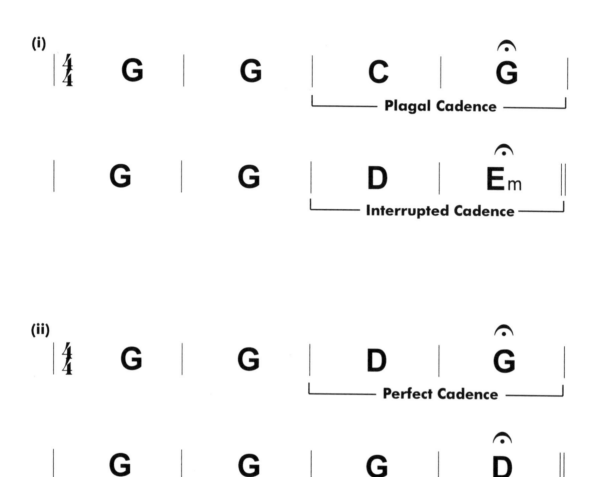

Example 2

♩. = 50

Example 3

♩ = 112

IMPROVISATION

An ability to improvise and come up with ad-libs is an important skill for a pop vocalist: some of the most exciting musical things happen when you 'work without the safety net'. To develop your skills in this area, listen to some of the ad-libs on the fade-outs of your CD/record collection, or expand your horizons by listening to some of the best jazz improvisers; sing along with the recordings and get a feel for what they're doing – then let go and do your own thing.

It's important that your improvisations fit the chords. Whilst studying before the exam, if you can play a chordal instrument (or can get someone to play one for you) practise slowly repeating a simple chord sequence until you get a real feel for the chord changes. Notice which notes work best over particular chords. At these grades, all the chords within each progression will be diatonic to the key, and so you can use the relevant key scale as the mainstay of your improvisation.

Whilst improvisation is not the same as composing a melody, an effective improvisation should contain clear evidence of melodic shaping and phrasing, as well as well-defined rhythmic and melodic motifs.

EXAM FORMAT

In the exam, the examiner will play a chord progression, in $\frac{4}{4}$ time, in a major or minor key, on a keyboard or guitar. This will be in the form of block chords, with a straightforward rhythmic groove. During the first playing the candidate should listen to the progression, before improvising over two further cycles of the progression.

The improvisation may be sung using any syllables, vowels, words or phrases of the candidate's choosing. Candidates may find it useful to come prepared with some memorised short lyric phrases which might be incorporated into the improvisation, however no extra marks will be awarded for any lyrics used and a 'scat' approach is perfectly acceptable.

IMPROVISATION – GRADE SIX

The examiner will play a chord progression of eight bars in length, which will contain two bars of each chord. Below are some examples of the *type* of chord progression that will be presented in this section of the examination.

Example 1

♩ = 120

| $\frac{4}{4}$ Am7 | Am7 | Dm7 | Dm7 |
| F | F | G | G ‖ |

Example 2

♩ = 138

| $\frac{4}{4}$ C | C | Am | Am |
| Dm | Dm | G7 | G7 ‖ |

Example 3

♩ = 144

| $\frac{4}{4}$ Cm | Cm | A♭maj7 | A♭maj7 |
| B♭ | B♭ | Fm | Fm ‖ |

IMPROVISATION – GRADE SEVEN

The examiner will play a chord progression of eight bars in length, which will contain one chord per bar. Below are some examples of the *type* of chord progression that will be presented in this section of the examination.

Example 1

♩ = 112

$\frac{4}{4}$ Cmaj7	Dm7	Em7	Fmaj7
Am7	Dm7	Em7	G ‖

Example 2

♩ = 132

$\frac{4}{4}$ Cm7	B♭	Fm7	Gm7
A♭	B♭	E♭	B♭ ‖

Example 3

♩ = 120

$\frac{4}{4}$ C7	F7	C	C7
G7	F7	C	G7 ‖

IMPROVISATION – GRADE EIGHT

The examiner will play a chord progression of twelve bars in length, which may contain up to two chords per bar. Below are some examples of the *type* of chord progression that will be presented in this section of the examination.

Example 1

♩ = 152

| $\frac{4}{4}$ C | G | Am | F | C | G |

| F / G / | C | F / G / | Am / Em / | F / G / | C ‖

Example 2

♩ = 116

| $\frac{4}{4}$ C7 | F7 | C | C7 | F7 | E♭ |

| C | C7 | G7 | F7 | C7 / F7 / | C7 / G7 / ‖

Example 3

♩ = 100

| $\frac{4}{4}$ Cm9 | Fm9 | Cm9 | A♭maj7 / B♭7 / | Fm7 | Gm / A♭ / |

| Fm7 | B♭ | Fm7 | Gm / A♭ / | E♭ | B♭ ‖

Conclusion

After having studied this handbook, anyone considering entering one of the London College of Music grade examinations in popular music vocals should note the following:

It is the candidate's responsibility to have knowledge of, and comply with, the current syllabus requirements. Where candidates are entered for examinations by teachers, the teacher must take responsibility that candidates are entered in accordance with the current syllabus requirements. Whilst all the information within this handbook was valid at the time of publication, it is important that candidates and teachers check that the contents of this handbook match the syllabus that is valid at the time of entry.